LIFEBOAT

Lifeboat

ALIE DAY

To all the lost and lonely souls who had the bravery and nerve to love relentlessly

Copyright © 2022 by Alie Day

All rights reserved. No part of this book may be reproduced in any manner whatsoever without written permission except in the case of brief quotations embodied in critical articles and reviews.

First Printing, 2022

Contents

Dedication   iv

Misfit	1
Falling	2
Quake	3
Bubblegum High	4
Nose to Nose	5
I-Never-Tability	6
Real	7
Happiness	8
It's You	9
Universe	10
Lifeboat Man	11
Let Go	12
Tumble	13
Living	14
Until Morning	15
Somehow	16

Everything	17
For Him	18
Giving up	19
Mistakes	20
Conflicted	21
Mirror Me	22
Letting Go	23
Escape	24
Hollow	25
Silence	26
For a Moment	27
Bed	28
Void	29
Raw	30
Tethered	31
Lost	32
Pause	33
Reality	34
Misery	35
About The Author	36
Acknowledgements	37

Misfit

We are not invincible
Our hearts aren't made of steel
Out skin is not unbreakable
And each of us can feel
The pain that is upon us
Whenever arrows hit
Spiteful tongues and flailing fists
Where none of us shall fit

Falling

I am Falling
And it's not slow
And it's not delicate
Stumbling through me
Into you
Clumsy and Catastrophic
But I'm me
Finally, I'm me
Falling
For you

Quake

I fell
Cliff-dive
Tumbling-alive
Toes first
Heart burst
Water quakes
And body shakes
I hit the surface
With a purpose
But then your hand upon my head
Fills my lungs with drowning dread
Flailing, thrashing
In the waves
You drowned me, darling
But that's okay.

Bubblegum High

Your hand on my thigh
Fingers entwined
Tongues grazing lips
On a bubblegum high
Arms around waists
Nose touching nose
Those gazes that wander
Keep me on my toes

Nose to Nose

Your hands holding my face
So close
Looking me in the eyes
Nose to nose
Your lips whispering your pride
Me believing it
For once
And then a kiss
Sealing fate
And I never want you
To let go of my face

I-Never-Tability

Never did I think a voice
Could calm the crashing waves of my soul
Never did I think one touch
Could demolish walls I had spent a lifetime securing
Never did I think
I would be so ready
To lose myself in another
And then there was you.
All of my "never's"
Became a distant memory

Real

And somehow
I'm no longer lost at sea
As silence falls
On you and me
And in these moments
Words are true
Even when you're feeling blue
And in your eyes
I find that we
Are more real than we
Meant to be

Happiness

I let it creep in;
Happiness, I mean.
Slowly, but surely
Building trust
Learning to fly again
With the gentle grazing of your lips;
These broken wings, repaired.

It's You

And I wonder
Frequently
Why I exist in this world
But it's you
It's you that calms my stormy sorrow
Accompanying my raucous mental thunder
With surges of bright white lightning
Destined to bring me home
Shock me back to life

Universe

I don't know why
Or how it happened
But somewhere, somehow
You became my universe
And now I'm afraid
Because it's okay
To lose something you never had a chance to know
But when you lose something you deeply care for
You lose yourself
Please don't let me lose
This time

Lifeboat Man

As the icy black tendrils
Of the night sky pull me under
You are all that is left of my sanity
As the darkest of thoughts
Tug at the edges of my mind
You are my paper boat
Throwing me a rope
Dragging me back on deck
As my heart bleeds
For losses I cannot forget
You are my lifeboat man
Always saving me
And when it's you
I want to be saved

Let Go

"Let go," he whispers
Into her neck
And she wants to
But the fear still grips her
Like the cold, dead hands of Christmas past
She knows she'll slip up
If she lets go, she'll say
"It"
And once she says it
There's no turning back

Tumble

It was that smile
The passion in his eyes
The way he wanted to know
Everything about the world
The same way I did
It was the softness in his voice
The roughness of his hands
The way he was in control
When I couldn't be in control
It was everything
The littlest things
That made me tumble
Aimlessly
For him

Living

His chest against her back
Arms stretched out
Fingers entwined
Softly breathing
Slowly drifting
No sign of fear
No nightmares here
This is it.
This
Is living

Until Morning

She could stare at his face for hours
Though she knew it by heart now
She would never tire of watching those eyes
Bore into her soul
She would never tire of the love that burned through her
At the sight and sound of him
Once afraid to get too close
Now only afraid
Of goodnight
Until morning

Somehow

Burnt out
Stressed out
Crying out
Freaking out
And by some miracle
Somehow you're still here
Somehow you know
Just what to say
To make me smile
To get me through the day
And somehow luck fell upon me with you
And I don't always understand
How I got this lucky
But I'm always grateful
For you

Everything

Everything I have
Everything I am
Is yours

For Him

For him
She would travel
To every corner of the world

For him
She would scour the universe
For the perfect star

For him
She would lay her fragile heart
On the line

Because For Him
It was worth it all

Giving up

Why does it matter
What you or I think?
We're destined for glory
Or doom
On the brink of knowing
And leaving
And fighting the same
You're giving up
On my "cannot be tamed"
So where do we stand
Sweetness and light?
You're already poised
To give up
This fight

Mistakes

If all these mistakes
Were notes on a stave
I'd compose you a symphony
From all that I've made
And if I could go back
And do it again
If I could close my eyes
And count to ten
To go back to the good
And stop the goodbyes
Oh darling, just let me
Close my eyes

Conflicted

Conflicted
Hearts and wars
And broken laws
And sticks and stones
And no one knows
Teeth and lips
And hands and hips
And love and life
A double edged knife
You and me
And those that flee
And hearts that break
And chances to take
And severed links
To show the chinks
In armour bound
By the restless sound
Of silence

Mirror Me

Why
When I look in the mirror
Do I hate her?

Letting Go

Letting go
Something I've always struggled with
Friends
Lovers
Enemies and memories
Why can't I let you go?

Escape

For once
I would just like
To fall asleep
And not have it feel
Like an excuse
To escape something

Hollow

I gave you everything you are
And left myself with nothing
But what have you
Now I am hollow?

Silence

Here is me
No longer powerful
Hinged upon the silence
Of a man

For a Moment

Just stop
If only for a moment
It's okay to be scared
Its okay to cry
Just stop
Smell the roses
Dance in the rain
If only for a moment

Bed

I roll onto your side of the bed
I feel your ghost there
The memory of you beside me
My head on your steady chest
My other half
My soulmate
Now there is only cold sheets
Silence and solitude
Pain and longing
But there I am
Holding on
To your side of the bed

Void

A void
My mind is a void
Fuzzy, dark and deep
Never ending
Tumbling
Like Alice
Down the rabbit hole
Down and down and down I go
Spiralling into the past
Hurtling towards the future
And pain is all I feel now
Tight
Constricting
A hand squeezing my heart so tightly it might burst
But I deal with it well
Because pain is all I know
And the happiness was a nice reprieve
For a while at least
Back down the rabbit hole
I go

Raw

I don't want to be drunk
I don't want to be numb
I don't even want to be in control
I want to feel this pain
This raw, itching, nagging pain
Because it's all I have left of you
And I want to hold onto you
Forever

Tethered

A string connects my heart to yours
Invisible, yet unbreakable
And when you're gone I feel it tug
Pulling me to you
Tugging
Pulling
Wrenching me towards you
Do you feel it too?

Lost

She lost a lot
Herself
Her love
A puzzle piece made of him
Made of her
Her whole world
Her Dreams
In an instant
Lost

Pause

If I could pause that moment
The moment you looked into my eyes
For the last time
And told me you loved me
The moment I turned away
Tears in my eyes
The pain unbearable
I would pause that moment
I would stare into your speckled green eyes
Forever

Reality

It became real that night
Mere guesses became truths
The walls she had built
Walls he had knocked down
Shot back up from the ground
like a fortress.

The trust she had put into him
The losses she had grieved
All while he had secrets
He desperately wanted to keep.

Reality set in that night
The love that she lost
Already stood with another
And she remained erased
From his heart
And from his memory

Misery

Sweet misery
Take away the sun and leave only moonlight
For it is all we deserve
Oh, apathy
Take away this passion
And leave only silence
For it only causes pain
Ignorance
Let me be blissful
And miss all the tragedy the world has to offer
Dutiful nature
Take away the honey
Take away the poison
Leave only earth
Let us start again

About The Author

Alie Day is a twenty-something author from southeast England. She is motivated, and stubborn and lets her impulse be her guide – it definitely gets her into trouble sometimes!

Alie used to work in the music industry and has since taken a different career path which she is extremely passionate about. She loves working hard and writes whenever she's not working. Music is still a huge part of her life, but she prefers the quiet, countryside lifestyle with her cats to the dark and scandalous world of the underground music scene.

Alie likes to read, write, and play her guitar in her spare time as well as embark on crafts she rarely has the time to finish. She's kooky, silly, and clumsy as anything and loves a good old natter at the end of a long day.

Alie loves traveling and photography and has embarked on some eye-opening and scenic journeys in her time on this planet.

You can find Alie here:
Instagram: @MissAlieWrites
Facebook: Alie Day Author
Twitter: @MissAlieWrites
www.AlieDay.co.uk

Acknowledgements

Here is the part where I thank a bunch of people and tell them how great they are, and the truth is, the people I'm about to name drop already know how special they are. Nothing I say could ever live up to quite how amazing the following people are and how much of an inspiration they have been to me...

Firstly, Mum and Dad. I may have to parent you half the time, but you have never left my side, have never judged me and have never let me give up on anything I am truly passionate about. I love you both to the moon and back, and without you and your support, I would never have been able to overcome the obstacles I've faced.

My little brother; you may be the village idiot and you may be younger than me, but I look up to you in ways you may never truly know and understand. Though you act like you're loosey goosey on the surface, I admire your compassion and your ability to say not what a person wants to hear, but what they need to hear. We've always had each other's backs and I'm forever grateful to have you in my corner.

Lily; you are a wonderful person who I know has been in my corner even when I thought I was there alone. I adore your ability to motivate people and pick them up when things are rough, even when you are trying to navigate life yourself. I appreciate you more than I could ever tell you.

Holly, Josh, Liv and Pabs; What would I do without you? Sometimes family are the people you choose and who choose you. I am so grateful to have you in my life, to know that I can call you family and watch yours grow and flourish into something beautiful. You guys inspire me every single day.

Rebecca; We have come a bloody long way and as you know, neither of us has had an easy ride. I am so, so proud of the person you have become and the achievements and successes you've had along the way. You remind me of better times and you remind me that as long as you are my friend, there will always be more good times on the horizon.

Sh'i'na; Where would I be without the girl I can talk to about obsessive TV habits and 80 & 90s cult classics? Your positivity is a ray of sunshine and I appreciate every moment that those positive rays of light have shone down on me in tough times.

My grandparents, aunts, uncles, cousins and extended family; without you, I wouldn't be the person I am today and I am grateful that you accept me as I am, quirks and all. You have allowed me to grow into the woman I am and though we may not see each other often, you are always in my thoughts and in my heart.

The Marchs and the Thompsons; Another extension of my family that I could not have grown without. You have seen the highs and the lows, given the best advice and always been on the end of the phone. I appreciate every one of you for the people you are and for the strength you have lent me over the years.

My pets; I love you with all my heart. There's nothing else to say except that you are my reason to smile every day.

And finally, to my readers. I am so grateful for your love and support. I hope this book and the poems within can provide the catharsis and shoulder to cry on that it provided me while I was writing it.

www.ingramcontent.com/pod-product-compliance
Lightning Source LLC
La Vergne TN
LVHW042004060526
838200LV00041B/1868